Cambridge Discovery Education™

▶ INTERACTIVE READERS

Series editor: Bob Hastings

TURTLES
ANCIENT SYMBOL / MODERN SURVIVOR

B2

Karmel Schreyer

CAMBRIDGE UNIVERSITY PRESS   Discovery EDUCATION™

CAMBRIDGE UNIVERSITY PRESS
Cambridge, New York, Melbourne, Madrid, Cape Town,
Singapore, São Paulo, Delhi, Mexico City

Cambridge University Press
32 Avenue of the Americas, New York, NY 10013-2473, USA

www.cambridge.org
Information on this title: www.cambridge.org/9781107660571

© Cambridge University Press 2014

This publication is in copyright. Subject to statutory exception and to the provisions of relevant collective licensing agreements, no reproduction of any part may take place without the written permission of Cambridge University Press.

First published 2014

Printed in Hong Kong, China, by Golden Cup Printing Company Limited

A catalog record for this publication is available from the British Library.

Library of Congress Cataloging-in-Publication Data

Schreyer, Karmel.
  Turtles : ancient symbol/modern survivor / Karmel Schreyer.
     pages cm. -- (Cambridge discovery interactive readers)
  ISBN 978-1-107-66057-1 (pbk. : alk. paper)
  1. Turtles--Juvenile literature. 2. English language--Textbooks for foreign speakers. 3. Readers (Elementary) I. Title.

QL666.C5S34 2013
597.92--dc23

2013024752

ISBN 978-1-107-66057-1

Additional resources for this publication at www.cambridge.org

Cambridge University Press has no responsibility for the persistence or accuracy of URLs for external or third-party Internet Web sites referred to in this publication and does not guarantee that any content on such Web sites is, or will remain, accurate or appropriate.

Layout services, art direction, book design, and photo research: Q2ABillSMITH GROUP
Editorial services: Hyphen S.A.
Audio production: CityVox, New York
Video production: Q2ABillSMITH GROUP

Contents

Before You Read: Get Ready! 4

CHAPTER 1
Turtle Basics 6

CHAPTER 2
Symbols and Significance 8

CHAPTER 3
Tortoises 14

CHAPTER 4
Freshwater and Sea Turtles 20

CHAPTER 5
What Do You Think? 24

After You Read 26

Answer Key 28

Glossary

Before You Read:
Get Ready!

Which animals on Earth today can be considered a cousin of the dinosaurs? Which animals carry their house with them wherever they go? Which may look ancient – and perhaps ugly, too – but are thought of as symbols of wisdom and goodness in traditional cultures everywhere? Turtles and tortoises are two amazing, and quite different, species of reptile. Let's learn more about them.

Words to Know

Read the species fact cards. Then complete the chart below.

Olive Ridley Turtle	This **species** of **reptile** loves its **swamp habitat**. The female uses her **flippers** to cover the eggs in her **nest**. The legs of these turtles are **adapted** to life in water.
Leopard Tortoise	This reptile loves its dry **savanna** habitat. Its heavy **shell** helps keep it cool. The female tortoise digs a nest with her claws to lay eggs. The eggs **hatch** about two months later.

Species	Olive Ridley Turtle	Leopard Tortoise
habitat	water, such as swamp	
main body	shell	shell
body parts		legs, claws
baby / place	eggs / nest	

Words to Know

Use the words in the box to complete the sentences.

adapt	habitat	nest	savanna	species
flippers	hatch	reptiles	shells	swamp

1. Turtles and tortoises are different, but they are both _____.

2. There are different _____ of turtle; some like sea water, some like fresh water.

3. Both turtles and tortoises have hard _____ that are a part of their body.

4. Tortoises have legs and feet with claws, but sea turtles have _____.

5. Tortoises live mostly on land. Some like a dry habitat, such as a _____.

6. Turtles like to live in a _____ with water, such as a _____.

7. Both turtles and tortoises lay eggs in a _____ in the soil or the sand.

8. They do not stay to watch the eggs _____.

9. Tortoises _____ to hot and cold temperatures; one way is by living in holes.

APPLY

Have you ever had a turtle or tortoise as a pet? What do you think about keeping reptiles as pets?

CHAPTER 1

Turtle Basics

TURTLES ARE AMONG THE OLDEST ANIMAL SPECIES STILL ALIVE. THEY ARE DEFINITELY THE OLDEST REPTILE.

We have evidence of turtles, found in ancient fossils,[1] dating as far back as 220 million years. They are great **survivors**, but they aren't just one thing. There are about 300 species of turtles, including tortoises.

They look similar, and people often use the word "turtle" for both animals, but there are big differences between turtles and tortoises. There are many similarities, too.

All turtle species, including sea turtles and tortoises, lay many eggs, and they lay them on land.

[1] **fossil:** part of a plant or animal, or its shape, that has been preserved in rock or earth for a very long period

Turtles	**Tortoises**
• live on land and in the sea	• are land animals
• are generally smaller than tortoises – from 7 to 100 cm in length	• are generally larger than turtles – up to 150 cm in length
• weigh 140 g to 500 kg	• weigh up to 300 kg
• can live for 100 years	• live up to 200 years
• have shells and legs that match the needs of their environment. Sea turtles have flippers instead of feet.	• have heavy shells and thick legs, which make them the slowest reptiles on Earth!

Unlike most mammal[2] species, neither turtles nor tortoises care for their young. Once an egg hatches, the baby is on its own!

Turtles and tortoises have **adapted** to **habitats** on all continents, except Antarctica. Some species live in tropical rainforests, whereas others live in dry savannas. Africa has the widest variety of turtle and tortoise species.

The diets of turtles and tortoises have adapted, too. Some eat meat, some eat plants, and some eat plants, animals, and insects. They both store food and water very well. Some species can live a year without eating or drinking!

[2]**mammal:** an animal that gives birth to babies, not eggs

CHAPTER 2

Symbols and Significance

THE TURTLE IS AN ANCIENT CREATURE. IT IS COUSIN TO THE DINOSAURS THAT ONCE WALKED OUR EARTH.

The turtle can help us imagine what our world must have been like before human beings ever lived. This long history, and the fact that turtles and tortoises can be found in almost all parts of the world, may explain why the turtle has played such a significant[3] role in so many cultures, both around the world and throughout history.

Turtles are often found in the traditional stories and songs of native people across North America, Asia, Africa, and South America. They are especially popular in China, Japan, Korea, and island cultures of the South Pacific.

[3] **significant:** important and meaningful

But no matter where the story or song comes from, there are interesting similarities in the **characteristics** of the turtle. It seems that, all around the world, turtle **symbolism** includes some of the characteristics we most admire in humans beings: innocence, patience, strength, steadiness, endurance, protectiveness, order, and wisdom.

For example, most people know the fable[4] of the tortoise and the hare, written by the ancient Greek storyteller Aesop. The fable is about a fast but arrogant hare that loses a race to a slow but determined turtle. "Slow and steady wins the race" is the message we take from this story. The message, of course, can be applied to life, too: concentrate on the job in front of you, avoid being careless and over-confident, and you will have success.

The tortoise beats the hare through patience and endurance.

The turtle can be found in more recent, but equally popular, literary works, too. English fantasy writer Terry Pratchett has written 40 novels in his series *Discworld*. His books take place on Discworld, a flat planet that sits on the backs of four enormous elephants. These elephants stand on the back of a giant turtle as it swims through space.

[4]**fable:** a short story that shows people how to behave

The idea of a world resting on elephants standing on the back of a turtle may seem fantastic and unique. But Pratchett did not invent it. He was inspired by a well-known Hindu creation myth (a story about the creation of the universe). In this story, the Earth is supported by elephants standing on the back of a turtle.

In fact, this idea is repeated in many other cultures. A turtle holding up the Earth and skies can also be found in Chinese stories. The rounded carapace, or top part of the shell, is a symbol of the heavens, and the plastron, the flat underside of the shell protecting the animal itself, is seen as the Earth.

Across the ocean, in the traditional cultures of North America, turtles and tortoises are also viewed as symbols of the creation of the world and the universe. In some of these creation myths, the turtle created Earth by collecting and piling up mud from the bottom of the sea. In others, the quietly reliable turtle offered his strong shell as the base on which all other animals could build their world.

The turtle also has other symbolic meanings. Because turtles live so long, they are viewed as a symbol of long life and the wisdom that comes from living for many years. In African children's stories, for example, the tortoise is always the cleverest character and likes to play tricks on others. Even in Western culture today, turtles in cartoons often wear glasses, a sign of being smart or a good student.

ANALYZE
Think of three other animals and the stories, fables, and myths they are part of. What are they symbols of?

The Korean Memorial Monument in Hiroshima Peace Park

Related to the idea of long life, the turtle is also viewed as a symbol of the afterlife, or life after death. In some Asian cultures, the turtle transports people from life to their afterlife when they die. In China and Korea, the turtle symbol is commonly used during funerals. Burial mounds[5] are also shaped like turtles.

At Hiroshima Peace Park, the Korean Memorial Monument, for Korean victims of the atomic bomb dropped on Hiroshima during World War II, is placed on a giant turtle.

[5] **burial mound:** a small hill where dead people are buried

And just to show how diverse turtle symbolism is, the turtle is also seen as a symbol of fertility[6] – the creation of life itself. Because female turtles produce many eggs at one time, turtles are admired as great creators. Chinese people look at the Black Tortoise as a good luck symbol for home and family life and strong relationships. And because of this symbolism, the turtle is a popular symbol on jewelry for women who wish to become pregnant and have babies.

There are a few cultures and historical periods in which the turtle is seen in a negative way, however. In ancient Greece, turtles were considered to come from hell.[7] During the Middle Ages in Europe, turtles were seen as evil. The ancient Aztecs in Central America saw turtles as boastful cowards.[8]

Whether they are loved or hated, feared or admired, one thing is sure: turtles have earned the respect of humans around the world and throughout time.

[6] **fertility:** the ability to make babies
[7] **hell:** the place where some people think bad people go when they die
[8] **coward:** someone who is afraid to do dangerous things

Video Quest

Symbolism

Watch this video to learn more about the symbolism of turtles. What culture holds the beliefs shown here?

CHAPTER 3

Tortoises

DID YOU KNOW A TORTOISE WENT TO THE MOON AND BACK BEFORE PEOPLE DID?

In 1968, the Soviet Union sent a Russian tortoise on a trip around the moon. Space is not, of course, a typical habitat for the tortoise, and neither is water. Unlike many species of turtle, tortoises live only on land. Except for drinking and bathing, tortoises stay away from water as much as possible. It is not surprising, then, that tortoises have thick, flat feet that can make their way over almost any type of ground.

Almost all tortoises are vegetarians, or herbivores. They eat a variety of grasses, leaves, fruits, and flowers. A few tortoise species, such as the Red-foot tortoise, are omnivores, which means they eat everything!

Although most tortoises do not eat meat, their bodies do provide meat for others. Baby tortoises especially are a favorite food for many other species.

People eat tortoises, too. During the Great Depression,[9] the Gopher tortoise of the southeastern United States was called "Hoover chicken," named after Herbert Hoover, who was the president at the time. In some cultures even today, however, the meat of tortoises is considered a delicacy.[10]

People may not eat tortoises very often, but they do keep them as pets. This means that the illegal trade in tortoises is growing. Many tortoise species are becoming endangered because of illegal trade.

Habitat destruction is another major factor that is leading to the declining numbers of tortoises throughout the world. If we are not careful, many tortoise species will disappear forever.

Currently, there are 40 different types of tortoise around the world. Let's look at a few of the most interesting ones.

[9]**The Great Depression:** the name for the period in US history, from 1929 to about 1940, when there was a huge drought (no rain) and also big economic problems

[10]**delicacy:** something rare or expensive that is good to eat

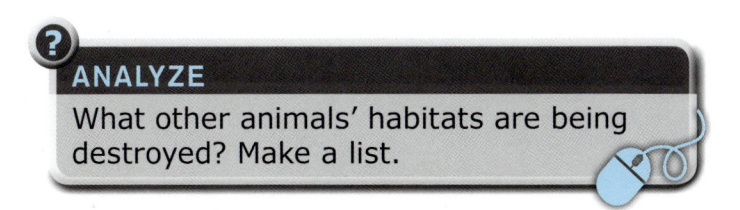

ANALYZE
What other animals' habitats are being destroyed? Make a list.

This tortoise (often wrongly called a turtle) is found in only two swamps in the world, both near Perth, Australia. It was once thought to be extinct; it hadn't been seen for 100 years. But then, in 1953, a student found one and brought it to a pet show. A scientist saw it there and took it to the Perth Zoo, where a **conservation** program was started immediately. The program is very successful, and now the zoo releases some western swamp tortoises into the wild every year!

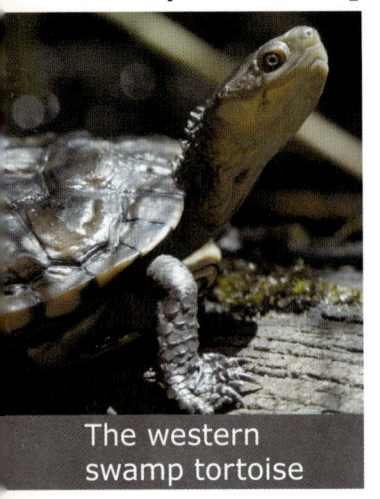

The western swamp tortoise

This tortoise lives in the savannas of Africa – just like real leopards. Its yellow shell has black spots, giving this tortoise its name.

The leopard tortoise

The African Pancake tortoise of east Africa is special because of its flat and flexible[11] shell, which allows the tortoise to squeeze between rocks for protection. Its shell is also very beautiful, making it a prize for zoos and private animal collections – and putting it on the list of endangered or nearly endangered species.

The African Pancake tortoise

[11] **flexible:** able to bend easily without breaking

The desert tortoise

This tortoise lives in the southwest United States and Mexico, where temperatures can reach 60°C. To survive, it digs burrows, or holes, under the ground, where it is cooler. These burrows also protect it from the cold at night. The desert tortoise spends up to 95 percent of its time underground, much of it in a dormant[12] state.

The largest living reptile on Earth! An adult can weigh 227 kilograms and can live for more than 150 years. The naturalist Charles Darwin was inspired by this animal when he visited the Galápagos Islands in 1835. The slight differences between the tortoises that lived on the mountainsides and the ones near the sea helped Darwin develop his ideas on how animals adapt to their environments. This led to his famous theory of evolution.

The Galápagos tortoise

[12] **dormant:** not active; sleeping for a long period

Video Quest

Galápagos Tortoise

Watch this video to learn more about this giant tortoise. What are some of its characteristics?

A tortoise of similar size to the Galápagos tortoise is the Aldabra tortoise, from the islands of the Aldabra Atoll in the Seychelles in the Indian Ocean. This chain of islands is home to over 100,000 of these giant tortoises.

The Aldabra tortoise became famous because of one particular tortoise, Mzee, and his unlikely friendship with a baby hippopotamus called Owen.

Haller Park in Kenya is an animal sanctuary, a place where endangered animals are protected. In December 2004, the park manager got a call about a baby hippopotamus in trouble. After a bad storm, the little hippo was stranded[13] on a tiny island off the coast of Kenya.

[13] **stranded:** not able to leave a place

The villagers living nearby asked Haller Park for help, and the manager there agreed to take the hippo. The villagers named the 300-kilogram baby Owen.

In December 2004, Mzee was about 130 years old. He was like a bad-tempered old man who didn't like to be around others. Then he met Owen.

Owen followed Mzee everywhere. He sat next to the big tortoise and rubbed his nose against Mzee's hard shell. Mzee moved away from Owen. Owen nuzzled[14] in closer.

Soon, Mzee and Owen became friends, and before long they were inseparable.[15] They ate together, swam together, and slept next to each other. Mzee taught Owen which leaves and plants were good to eat. When Mzee needed help climbing over something, Owen gave him a little push.

Owen and Mzee lived together until Owen became fully adult. Then, the park decided Owen needed to be with other hippos. Mzee is once again happily living on his own in the park. Owen now lives with a female hippo called Cleo.

[14] **nuzzle:** touch, rub, or press someone gently and affectionately, especially with the head or nose
[15] **inseparable:** such good friends that they are always together

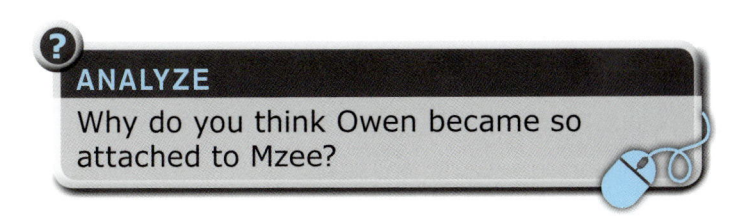

ANALYZE
Why do you think Owen became so attached to Mzee?

The Stinkpot turtle

The alligator snapping turtle

CHAPTER 4

Freshwater and Sea Turtles

LET'S LOOK AT SOME OF THE MANY TYPES OF FRESHWATER AND SEA TURTLES.

With their streamlined bodies and flippers instead of legs, freshwater and sea turtles are perfectly adapted to a life in the water.

The smallest freshwater turtle, the Stinkpot turtle, grows to no more than 12 centimeters long and weighs only about 600 grams. It gets its name from the terrible smell it produces as a way to protect itself from **predators**.

The largest freshwater species, the alligator snapping turtle, grows to an average weight of 80 kilograms and length of 66 centimeters. As you can guess from its sharp teeth, this species is a meat-eater. But it doesn't hunt its food; the food comes to it.

Inside its mouth this turtle has a small, thin piece of skin that looks like a little worm. The turtle opens its mouth and a fish sees the skin moving around and thinks it is a worm. The fish swims into the turtle's mouth to get the worm, then SNAP! Dinner for the turtle!

The olive ridley is a small species, usually growing to no more than 70 centimeters in length and 50 kilograms in weight. They are found in the Atlantic, Pacific, and Indian oceans, and one of their most interesting characteristics is how they reproduce.[16]

Olive ridley sea turtles

Many female olive ridley turtles come to one particular beach at one time to lay their eggs. Each turtle makes a nest by digging a hole in the sand. Then, it lays 50–100 eggs and covers them again with sand to protect them. Two or three months later, thousands of baby turtles climb out of the sand and hurry down the beach to the sea. But not all of them get there.

[16] **reproduce:** make babies

Video Quest

Arribada

Watch this video to learn more about the olive ridley *arribada*, or nesting time. When do the females lay their eggs?

The leatherback sea turtle

All sea turtle species have hard, bone-like shells, except for the leatherback. Its carapace is soft and flexible, an adaptation that makes deep-water diving possible. A leatherback can dive as deep as 1,280 meters and stay under water for as long as an hour and a half.

Just like the tortoise, sea turtles are also suffering from falling numbers. The Kemp's ridley species, only found near a small coastal area in Mexico, is the most endangered sea turtle species in the world. But many other species, including the olive ridley and the leatherback, are also in trouble. In total, about half of all freshwater turtle species are threatened – that's more than any other animal on Earth!

The threats to sea turtles are both natural and man-made. Natural predators like crabs, birds, and fish catch the newly hatched turtles as they make their way into the water for the first time. Now, conservation groups around the world guard nesting grounds to help increase the turtles' chances of survival. But this work does not protect the turtles from their worst enemy.

Man is the greatest threat to sea turtles. People hunt them illegally. Fishers accidentally trap them in fishing nets. The waters where they live are increasingly polluted and filled with plastic garbage, which can hurt or kill the turtles if they eat it.

Another man-made threat is light pollution. When baby olive ridley turtles hatch at night, the light of the moon guides them to the sea. But the artificial lights from nearby villages and seaside hotels confuse them. They sometimes go in the wrong direction and are eaten by land animals or die under the wheels of cars. Conservation groups are working with local businesses to control the use of lighting during hatching times.

CHAPTER 5
What Do You Think?

TURTLES AND TORTOISES ARE AN IMPORTANT SYMBOL IN ANCIENT CULTURES, BUT THEY CONTINUE TO BE POPULAR IN MODERN CULTURE.

Turtles and tortoises have had a long relationship with humans. We find them in prehistoric cave paintings and Native American totem poles, but we also commonly find them in today's cartoons, comic books, literature, movies, and advertisements.

There's the popular children's storybook *Yertle the Turtle* by Dr. Seuss. Students at the University of Maryland in the United States are called the Terrapins (after a local turtle species). And do you remember the *Teenage Mutant Ninja Turtles*?

Turtles and tortoises have always held our fascination. Perhaps this is because they are mysterious and so different from us. But, as with many animals, even though they are different from us, we often use their characteristics to describe people or actions.

Look at these English idioms. What do you think they mean?

- His bark is worse than his bite.
- She's the black sheep of the family.
- My teacher will go ape if I hand in my paper late again.
- Hold your horses! I'll be there in a minute.
- He said he was sorry and that he wouldn't do it again, but a leopard can't change its spots.

What idioms or expressions do you know that use animal characteristics? Make a chart like the one below with some examples from English or your own language translated into English.

Idiom	Animal characteristics	Meaning
His bark is worse than his bite.	barking, biting (dog)	He sounds frightening, but he doesn't really do anything.

After You Read

Choose the Correct Answers

Read the sentences and choose Ⓐ, Ⓑ, Ⓒ, or Ⓓ.

1 Approximately how long have turtles been on the Earth?
- Ⓐ five thousand years
- Ⓑ one million years
- Ⓒ two hundred million years
- Ⓓ five hundred million years

2 Turtles and tortoises are closely related to which other animals?
- Ⓐ dolphins and whales
- Ⓑ dinosaurs
- Ⓒ monkeys and humans
- Ⓓ all four-legged animals

3 What is the main message from the fable of the tortoise and the hare?
- Ⓐ Don't think, just run.
- Ⓑ Everyone should try to run faster.
- Ⓒ Slow and steady wins the race.
- Ⓓ Take care of animals.

4 What are turtles and tortoises NOT a symbol of?
- Ⓐ cleverness
- Ⓑ fertility
- Ⓒ stupidity
- Ⓓ the afterlife

5 What was the first animal sent into space?
- Ⓐ a dog
- Ⓑ a monkey
- Ⓒ a turtle
- Ⓓ a tortoise

6 Which tortoise species lives in Australia?
- (A) Gopher tortoise
- (B) Western swamp tortoise
- (C) Leopard tortoise
- (D) Pancake tortoise

7 What did naturalist Charles Darwin write after seeing the Galápagos tortoise?
- (A) a dictionary about animals
- (B) *Discworld*
- (C) a book of fables
- (D) the theory of evolution

8 Which is the worst threat to the turtle?
- (A) light pollution
- (B) habitat destruction
- (C) man
- (D) predators such as crabs, birds, and larger fish

True or False?

Circle T (true) or F (false) for each statement.

1 Tortoises do not live as long as turtles.	T	F
2 Turtles are considered to be smart.	T	F
3 The carapace of a shell is the top part.	T	F
4 Burial mounds are shaped like turtles.	T	F
5 Owen and Mzee are a tortoise and a rhino.	T	F

Animal Pairs

Look at these pairs of animals. How are they alike? How are they different?

alligator / crocodile	lion / tiger
ape / monkey	mouse / rat
donkey / mule	rabbit / hare
butterfly / moth	frog / toad

Answer Key

Words to Know, page 4
habitat: water, such as swamp; land, such as savanna
main body: shell; shell
body parts: flippers; legs
baby/place: eggs/nest; eggs/nest

Words to Know, page 5
1 reptiles **2** species **3** shells **4** flippers **5** savanna
6 habitat; swamp **7** nest **8** hatch **9** adapt

Apply, page 5   *Answers will vary.*

Analyze, page 11   *Answers will vary.*

Video Quest, page 13
The people of southwestern Japan hold the beliefs shown in this video.

Analyze, page 15   *Answers will vary.*

Video Quest, page 17
Characteristics: hatched from eggs, small at birth; grows to great size and weight; has large, column-like legs

Analyze, page 19   *Answers will vary.*

Video Quest, page 21
They lay their eggs as the sun sets.

Choose the Correct Answers, page 26
1 C **2** B **3** C **4** C **5** D **6** B **7** D **8** C

True or False?, page 27
1 F **2** T **3** T **4** T **5** F

Animal Pairs, page 27   *Answers will vary.*